Extreme LIFE Cycles

CICADA

WRITTEN BY E.C. ANDREWS

KidHaven PUBLISHING

Published in 2025 by
KidHaven Publishing, an Imprint of
Greenhaven Publishing, LLC
2544 Clinton St., Buffalo, NY 14224

© 2024 BookLife Publishing Ltd.

Written by: E.C. Andrews
Edited by: Noah Leatherland
Designed by: Amelia Harris

All facts, statistics, web addresses and
URLs in this book were verified as valid and
accurate at time of writing. No responsibility
for any changes to external websites or
references can be accepted by either the
author or publisher.

Cataloging-in-Publication Data

Names: Andrews, E.C.
Title: Cicada / E.C. Andrews.
Description: Buffalo, New York : KidHaven
    Publishing, 2025. | Series: Extreme life cycles |
    Includes glossary and index.
Identifiers: ISBN 9781534546981 (pbk.) | I
    SBN 9781534546998 (library bound) |
    ISBN 9781534547001 (ebook)
Subjects: LCSH: Cicadas--Juvenile literature. |
    Cicadas--Life cycles--Juvenile literature.
Classification: LCC QL527.C5 A537 2025 |
    DDC 595.7'52--dc23

Manufactured in the United States of America

CPSIA compliance information: Batch #CSKH25
For further information contact Greenhaven Publishing LLC
at 1-844-317-7404.

Please visit our website,
www.greenhavenpublishing.com.
For a free color catalog of all our high-quality
books, call toll free 1-844-317-7404
or fax 1-844-317-7405.

Find us on

IMAGE CREDITS

CONTENTS

Words that look like this can be found in the glossary on page 24.

WHAT IS A LIFE CYCLE?

All living things grow throughout their lives. As they grow, they change. These changes make up different stages in their lives. This is called a life cycle.

BABY

CHILD

TEENAGER

ELDERLY PERSON

ADULT

Living things grow up, get old, and one day, they die. During their lives, some living things have <u>offspring</u>. Having offspring allows the life cycle to continue.

WHAT IS A CICADA?

A cicada is type of <u>insect</u>. There are over 3,000 known <u>species</u> of cicadas. Some cicadas have black and orange markings. Some cicadas have green markings. This helps them blend in with their surroundings.

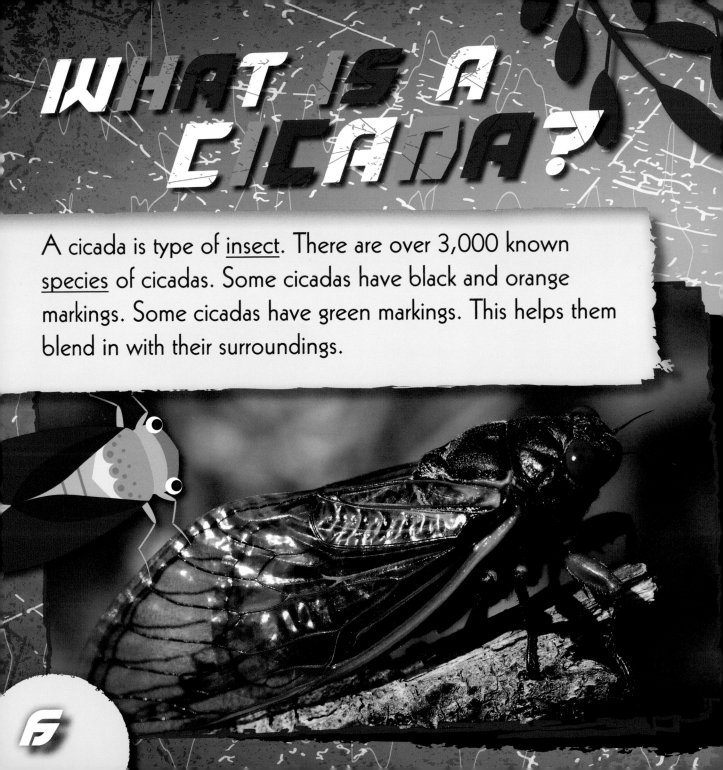

Cicadas usually live in forest areas. They mostly eat roots and tree <u>sap</u>, so they need to live near lots of trees. They need to eat a lot when they are young in order for them to grow.

LAYING THE EGGS

Female cicadas lay their eggs inside tree branches. All female cicadas have a long, sharp tube called an ovipositor. They use this to slice open tree branches so they can lay their eggs inside.

OVIPOSITOR

SLIT MADE BY A FEMALE CICADA

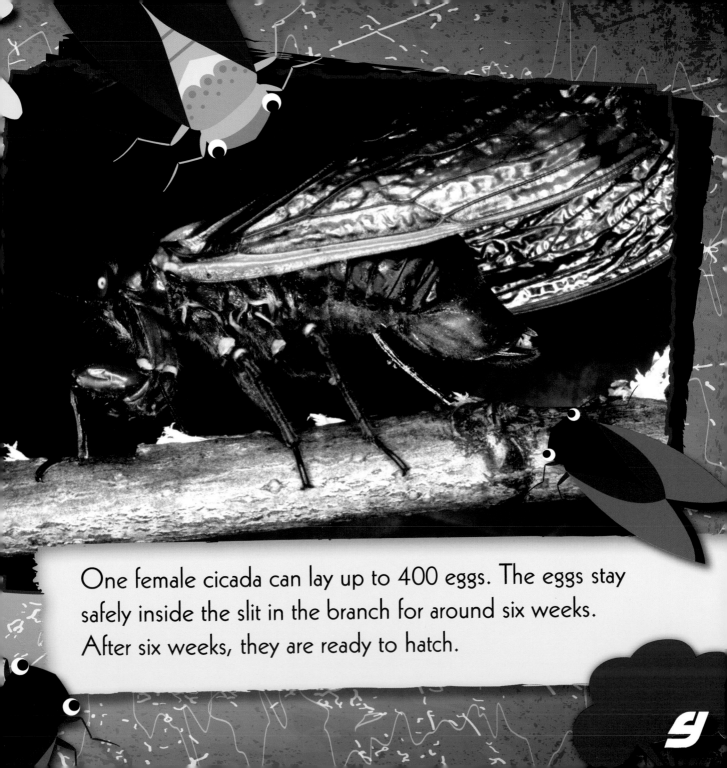

One female cicada can lay up to 400 eggs. The eggs stay safely inside the slit in the branch for around six weeks. After six weeks, they are ready to hatch.

HATCHING

Baby cicadas are called nymphs. When the nymphs hatch, they fall off the tree and onto the ground. Cicada nymphs are very light, so they are not hurt by the fall.

A NEWLY HATCHED NYMPH GETTING READY TO DIG

When the nymphs fall onto the ground, they start to dig right away. Cicada nymphs have sharp, hooked feet which help them dig through dirt and soil very quickly.

LIFE UNDERGROUND

Cicada nymphs dig until they find roots. When they are young, they feed on the sap from grass roots. As they grow, they feed on bigger roots from trees.

NYMPH EATING SAP FROM ROOTS

BURROWS MADE BY CICADA NYMPHS

Cicada nymphs live in underground tunnels for most of their lives. Some cicada species stay underground for two to four years. Others stay underground for up to 17 years!

NYMPHS EMERGE

After spending years underground, the nymphs <u>emerge</u> when the temperature is just right. This happens during the spring and summer seasons. Nymphs tunnel out of the ground and climb up the nearest plant.

AN ADULT CICADA SHEDDING ITS EXOSKELETON

The cicada nymphs hook their feet into the plant. This keeps them stable as they start to shed their exoskeleton. They emerge from their old exoskeletons as adult cicadas.

NEW WINGS

The empty nymph shells are often left clinging to plants. The adult cicadas now have wings and will soon be able to fly. First, they need some time to adjust to their new body.

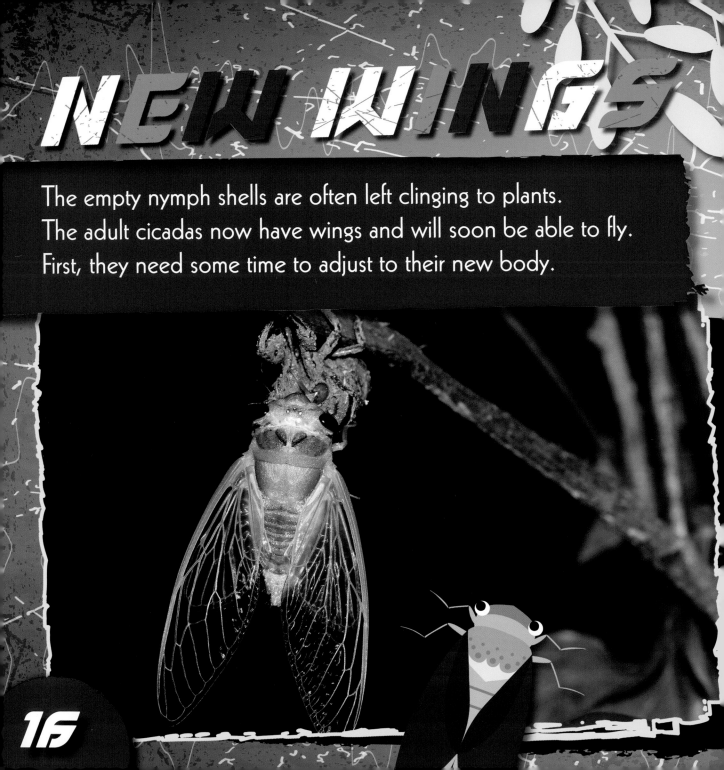

ADULT CICADA

EXOSKELETON

Cicada wings are small and dry when they first emerge from their nymph exoskeleton. Adult cicadas wait by their exoskeleton while their new wings grow strong enough for flight. This can take a few days.

SINGING

Adult male cicadas spend most of their time singing. Cicadas are one of the loudest insects in the world. The male cicadas sing to <u>attract</u> female cicadas so they can <u>reproduce</u> … and it works!

The females reply to the song by flicking their wings. This makes a loud clicking noise. The sound helps the male find the female. Then, they get ready to lay eggs.

END OF LIFE

Cicadas come and go in very large numbers.
They can be a good source of food for other animals.
A lot of them get caught and eaten.

The adult cicadas that survive long enough will reproduce. Adult cicadas only live for a few weeks. However, cicadas spend so long underground that they have some of the longest lives of any insects.

THE CYCLE CARRIES ON

Adult cicadas' top goal is to reproduce. They begin looking for a partner right away. Adult cicadas sing their songs to attract mates and allow the life cycle to carry on.

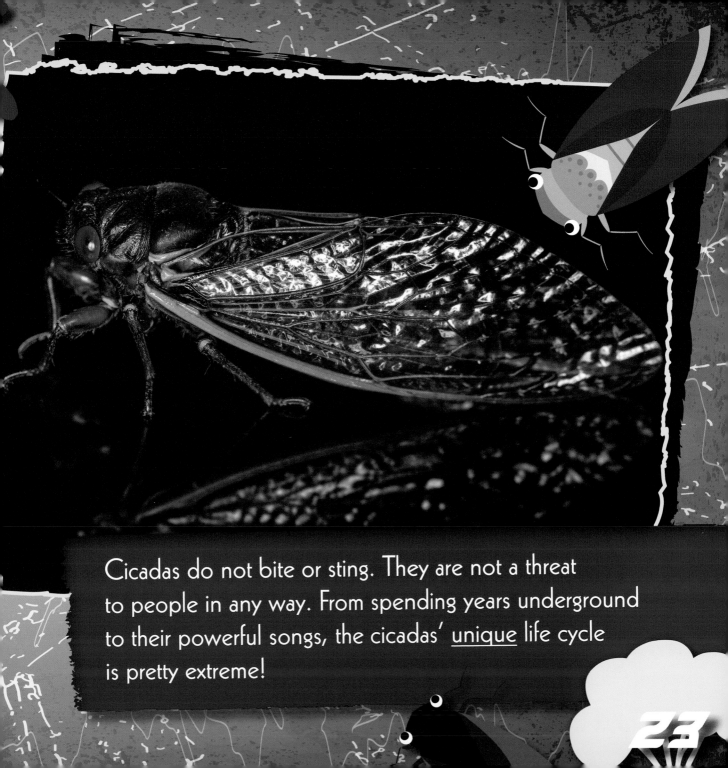

Cicadas do not bite or sting. They are not a threat to people in any way. From spending years underground to their powerful songs, the cicadas' <u>unique</u> life cycle is pretty extreme!

GLOSSARY

ATTRACT	to draw in
EMERGE	to come out of something
EXOSKELETON	the hard outer covering of some animals, like insects
INSECT	an animal with six legs and three body parts
OFFSPRING	the young of an animal or plant
REPRODUCE	to have offspring
SAP	a liquid found inside plants
SPECIES	a group of very similar animals or plants that can create young together
STABLE	secure and unlikely to break or come loose
UNIQUE	one of a kind, unlike anything or anyone else

INDEX